SQL

Complete guide to master SQL programming and data manipulation

Table of content

Introduction-

I want to congratulate you for reading this book, it will represent the best source of information that you can have on learning SQL and how to work with databases. If you are looking to improve your programming skills and get to the next level professionally that you made the right decision.

 You have in front of you a book that offers you a change, a book that will teach you vital information's on the fundamentals of database programming. Through the guidance that I will give you through this book you will have in the shortest time possible a better understanding of SQL language. As you will start reading you will see that I will present you step-by-step instructions either you are a beginner or experimented programmer.

It's no secret that more and more people are looking to the IT industry, to get into programming, web development, applications development, internet marketing, database manipulation and design. Taking the decision to become a database professional will be something that will define your career and will give you a secure job and also a big satisfaction for the work that you are doing.

We have to talk also about the salary. Every programmer should take that in consideration because it's a job usually with high remuneration. I can say that a good database programmer in United States it's being paid with over $ 100,000 USD per year. Chose your career wisely, chose it with attention and passion.

Thank you again for downloading this book. It will represent the best source that you need for learning SQL programming to the ultimate level. I hope you enjoy it!

Chapter 1 - SQL Overview

Why should you read this book?

If you are on your way to become a programmer (in any programming language) you should definitely study this book and add SQL to your "portfolio" of knowledge.

Time for fun! The best tools for keeping track of new things that are invented are databases so be careful to have this in mind. In this book will approach and discuss the following subjects :

- SQL Fundamentals and basics of SQL programming
- The Components of SQL
- How to get started with databases and database fundamentals
- How to take SQL to the real world
- Protect a database
- Determine how to get the information that you are interested in out of a database
- And much many other information's

SQL (Structured Query Language) is a domain specific language that is used for programming purposes and also for managing data that is being held in a *relational database management system* (RDBMS).

SQL mainly it's being used for creating databases, for simple actions like adding new data information's in them and also they are being used to maintain that held in them and give back to the programmer selected parts of the data selected. As many other great inventions of XX-s century, SQL , it's being developed originally by IBM in the 1970s. Since the moment of release till now SQL has grown a lot and developed as years went by to be at the industry standard.

The relational model is the model that SQL followed originally when it was designed by IBM. Nowadays the international SQL has incorporated the *object model.* By the end of this chapter will also see how data storage plays a big role in SQL world and will take a look on the most important features of relational databases.

Let's talk about databases

So what is a database? That is the main question that you have right now. Well the term database is something that is loosing the original meaning. Databases in some situations could mean just a collection of informations of a collection of data items. When we are saying data items we can talk about a list of e-mails, list of people to contact, any information that requires to be collected and held in a specific form.

Database definition: A database is representing a collection of data. A database can be a collection of tables, reports and lists. A database represents a model of different aspects of reality.

Short info

DBMS = Database management system is representing a computer software applications that interacts with the user and the purpose of this is to define, create, update, and administrate databases. When we are talking about DBMS we are talking about MySQL (often a misunderstanding is being made with SQL when people hear about MySQL. Also MySQL is representing a RDBMS – open source relational database management system and it's originally developed by MySQL AB), PostgreSQL, Microsoft SQL Server, Oracle, SAP HANA.

DBMS programs can easily be found on the market today, they don't run just on large computers or servers, they also can run on notebooks, tablets very easily. Due to the fact that technology it's developing at such a high speed we see a trend developing around the idea that storing data in the cloud it's the next big thing(well actually already begun being "the next big thing" and probably the future of data storing).Big companies like Google, Apple, Amazon have already implemented those type of technology for their business and even started offering cloud solutions for their customers.

Databases are defined by data and *metadata* (Metadata = data that describes and provides information's about other data. Metadata is descriptive, structural, administrative *)*

Due to the fact that databases have their descriptive nature we can say that databases are *self-describing*. Databases stores metadata in a "storage place" called *data dictionary* that it's being composed by the following : columns, constraints and other databases specific elements.

How big and complex are databases?.

A database will come in a lot form and sizes. Starting with simple and basic Excel tables to the most complex documents that you can imagine with thousands and millions of records (documents that are being used for example for "big data" purposes also). Databases can be categorized in the following: categorized by size of the database itself, categorized by the size of database and the size of the organization that it's holding it (Here, we can talk about :

- a personal database which is developed by an individual (single purposes) and as the name says it's being used for personal purposes. Generally, those type of databases are considered small databases they don't hold lots and lots of information's and usually being used to keep evidence of different things that the owner is interested in

- an enterprise database which is developed for enterprises and companies. The purpose of an enterprise databases is to model information and usually are huge databases. This type of databases contains information's about the entire company starting with the salaries of the employees and finishing with administrative information's about company maintenance.

    - a sectorial or departmental database that it's being used by small companies (10-20-30 employees) to keep evidence of activity or it's used by big companies by a hole sector. This type of database is in general pretty complex and the data must be handled by multiple users.

Relational Database

    When talking about relational databases it's important to talk about flexibility. You can add data in a table, you can delete data or change it in any way you want without modifying the relationship between other parts of the table.

    Relations database is composed of one or more relations. In general people are used to work with two-dimensional arrays of rows and columns(relation = two-dimensional array of rows and columns having single-valued entries).

    Tables can have columns and rows and just some of them help you in what you are doing. To get rid of data that you are not interested in just have to create a "*view*".

    Additional structures it's a necessity for a database to maintain control and stability.

Structures or schemas assures organization of a database. **Schemas** or conceptual view is representing how an entire database it's being organized when it's first created. Schemas it's the foundation of a database and it's mandatory in this process. We can also call it "logical view".

    Domains another relational element to a database is representing an element that describes that fact that there are finite numbers of values(ex: a column of a table it's representing a finite number of values).

Constraints are representing another relational element of a database. Constraints are being used to determine what values to enter in your table or not. Constraints are rules implemented to keep order in a table. For example the fact that people entering new data in your database can enter wrong values.

Database design considerations

It's very clear that a database it's basically a representation of a physical product or structure(let's say for example an automobile assembly or a house structure or performance for a team's players). Having a structure in place will help a lot, but also we have to keep in mind that accuracy of the representation it's very important. The level of details of the design that the database has and the amount of the effort that is put into the database design are correlated and depend totally on the amount of information and the type of information that you want to get out of that database.

! Before starting to work on your project please have in mind that it's very important to decide from the beginning the level of details you want your database to have in order to create the exact level of details in your design(it's very important to use exactly the details that you need for better results).

Nowadays database management systems are being made with a very very attractive graphic interface for a better experience for the user but also for the programmer that it's designing the database. They have a very attractive user interface for the user with intuitive design tools. Database design can be difficult sometimes, doing it wrong will affect your performance for sure, devote time and energy into it and will make tasks like data entry very easy to complete.

Did you know that?

Quick info, let's dive a little bit more into SQL history. As we said SQL was originally developed by IBM in their research laboratories. 1970 it's the year of birth of this important piece in database world where as we talked, DBMS (or RDBMS) relations systems were developed and called everything a data sublanguage. When they originally released SQL they called it "SEQUEL" and it stands for Structured English Query Language. The product was ready, everything was done and at the moment of release IBM encountered trademark problems. Another company has already named a product of them "SEQUEL" and they came with the name that all of us knows, SQL, marketing solutions as usual that are found by mistake and stand better than the original idea, to the first time when you can talk about something like.

Did you know that SQL doesn't stand for anything? Yes, that's true, SQL in reality doesn't stand for "structured query language" as it is presented everywhere (even though for not making any mistakes about it would be better to present it like that). It's just a sequence of 3 letters, also like C programming language that also doesn't stand for anything.

When IBM started working on SQL and relational databases they already were well known in IT industry. By that time that company that is now known as Oracle Corporation (Relational Software) was releasing their first RDBMS and also IBM was in 1981 and the competition between those two as been created. IBM products extended in short time and took a bigger piece of the market.

Chapter 2: SQL Fundamentals

At the end of this chapter you will be able to:

- Have a basic understanding of SQL language
- How to put SQL to wok with a server system
- Have a better understanding of different SQL standards
- Be familiar with SQL commands
- Be familiar with how to represent numbers, dates, times and other data types
- Explore null values and many other useful information's

SQL is easy to use!

SQL it's pretty easy to use due to the fact that it's a very flexible language (not talking about the fact that it's also pretty easy to learn) and it can be used in many many ways with different approaches. One of the most frequent purposes of this (non-procedural) language is for communicating with relational databases.

From the beginning of this chapter I want to make something clear: SQL its not a procedural language like C, C++, Java and other programming languages. However due to the fact that lots and lots of programmers are used to solve problems in a procedural way often this mistake it's being made about SQL. Recently there was been a try to add more procedural functionalities to SQL because of the the way that the language it's being used. As a result of this finally has been added a couple of procedural features like: BEGIN, IF /ELSE statements, also functions and not to forget about procedures, with those features added SQL it's facilitating now storing programs on the servers.

Let's talk about **queries.** A query is a statement/ question / affirmation you ask to the database. After asking , if there is any data in your database that completes the request or satisfies the conditions of your query, SQL will retrieve(return) that data you asked for. It's basically a confirmation to your request question – action. Those type of features make SQL to look and feel more and more like a programming language but still a lot of features are missing and its pretty far from meeting basic requirements of a programming language and fundamentals to many other languages. Applications developed and used in real world require use of a programming language and this is one of the reasons that SQL it's called a *data sublanguage.*

How to extract informations from a database

To exact information's from a database it's pretty simple, as a matter a fact there are two ways to do it. One of the ways you can exact information's it's the following:

- Create an "ad hoc" query just by typing from keyboard an SQL statement. Those type of query reaction to extract information's are used because they are very good for receiving a quick answer. This is a solution used when you want a fast response to your requirement and to meet an immediate need (that also will require information's never used in your database)

The second way that we are going to approach for extracting information's from your database it's by:

- Executing a program that collects information's from the database and immediately after that to create reports on the information(onscreen or printed). Here we can talk about the fact that adding an SQL query direct to the program you are working with is a very good way to run that query in a complex way.

SQL Statements

Here is where the fun begins. SQL differentiates from other languages by the fact that has a limited number of statements that perform three functions of data handling: a type of functions defines data, another type of functions manipulates data and the third type of functions just have to control data.

SQL implemented in 2011 , SQL: 2011, a basic set of core features. They also include extensions to the core set and a couple of comments are being specified in the following table.

ADD	DEALLOCATE PREPARE	FREE LOCATOR
ALLOCATE CURSOR	DECLARE	GET DESCRIPTOR
ALLOCATE DESCRIPTOR	DECLARE LOCAL TEMPORARY TABLE	GET DIAGNOSTICS
ALTER DOMAIN	DELETE	GRANT PRIVILEGE
ALTER ROUTINE	DESCRIBE INPUT	GRANT ROLE
ALTER SEQUENCE GENERATOR	DESCRIBE OUTPUT	HOLD LOCATOR
ALTER TABLE	DISCONNECT	INSERT
ALTER TRANSFORM	DROP	MERGE
ALTER TYPE	DROP ASSERTION	OPEN
CALL	DROP ATTRIBUTE	PREPARE
CLOSE	DROP CAST	RELEASE SAVEPOINT
COMMIT	DROP CHARACTER SET	RETURN
CONNECT	DROP COLLATION	REVOKE
CREATE	DROP COLUMN	ROLLBACK
CREATE ASSERTION	DROP CONSTRAINT	SAVEPOINT
CREATE CAST	DROP DEFAULT	SELECT
CREATE CHARACTER SET	DROP DOMAIN	SET CATALOG
CREATE COLLATION	DROP METHOD	SET CONNECTION
CREATE DOMAIN	DROP ORDERING	SET CONSTRAINTS
CREATE FUNCTION	DROP ROLE	SET DESCRIPTOR
CREATE METHOD	DROP ROUTINE	SET NAMES
CREATE ORDERING	DROP SCHEMA	SET PATH
CREATE PROCEDURE	DROP SCOPE	SET ROLE
CREATE ROLE	DROP SEQUENCE	SET SCHEMA
CREATE SCHEMA	DROP TABLE	SET SESSION AUTHORIZATION
CREATE SEQUENCE	DROP TRANSFORM	SET SESSION CHARACTERISTICS
CREATE TABLE	DROP TRANSLATION	SET SESSION COLLATION
CREATE TRANSFORM	DROP TRIGGER	SET TIME ZONE
CREATE TRANSLATION	DROP TYPE	SET TRANSACTION
CREATE TRIGGER	DROP VIEW	SET TRANSFORM GROUP
CREATE TYPE	EXECUTE IMMEDIATE	START TRANSACTION
CREATE VIEW	FETCH	UPDATE
DEALLOCATE DESCRIPTOR		

Those are the most important statements that you are going to use when programming in SQL but in addition to that there are a couple of statements that have a special role in SQL world. Those are being reserved for specific actions and can be used in different ways from their intent of use.

Lets talk about **data types.** During the history IBM implemented to SQL different types of data types so would make the language opened for more actions and able to generate more results. Here are the predefined general types that SQL recognizes :

- Strings
- Binary
- Numerical
- Intervals
- Booleans
- XML
- Data times

Every type of data generates several subtypes like numerics, approximate numerics, bit strings, character strings, large object strings. Also SQL supports user-defined types and constructed types.

Exact numerics

" Extract numeric" data types enables you to express the value of a number exactly. Here we talk about 5 data types :

- Integer
- Small int
- Big int
- Numeric
- Decimal

Integer data type has no fractional part, it's precision depends on SQL implementation.

Small INT data type it also can be used with integers but his precision in implementation can't get larger than Integer on the same implementation.

BIG INT data type is a type of data that has the precision as great as Integer type. Also the precision of BIG INT data depends on implementation.

Numeric data type represents a type of data that has a fractional component and in addition to its integer component. You can have both the precision and the scale of Numeric data just by specifying it.

The decimal data type is similar to Numeric data type. The decimal data type can have a fractional component and this data type can be specified the precision and the scale. The difference that we have here is that in the implementation process you might have to specify a precision greater than what you specify .

REAL data type gives to the user a single-precision floating point-number which also depends on SQL implementation. A 64-bit computer for example will give you more better precision than a 32-bit computer, that means also that the hardware you use also determines precision.

DOUBLE precision data type represents a data type that gives you a double precision floating point number so that means that the precision will again depend on the implementation process. Even though may sounds complicated and pretty scary at first the only purpose of the word "double" here is just to accentuate that everything it's based on the process of implementation.

FLOAT data type can be described as the most useful data type in case you need to migrate your database from a hardware platform with register sizes different from the platform data your database is currently on.

Character Strings are described best as graphic images, sounds, pictures or even little animations. We have a couple of main categories for Character data:

- Fixed character data
- Character large-object data
- Variable character data

And a couple of subcategories:

- National Character
- National character variable
- National character large object

Character data type is a type where you define a data type of a column as Character or Char having the possibility to specify the number of characters the column holds.

Character Variable data type is very useful if we have a situation where entries in a column vary in length and you don't want SQL to have any empty fields. This lets you store the number of characters that your user wants to enter.

Character large object data type is a type of data that was originally introduced with SQL:1999. Character large object data type it's used for a very large character string that can't be used with Character type.

Binary strings were originally introduced with SQL:2008 so the "update" was relatively recent introduced by IBM. The binary data has been fundamental to digital computers and seems like a little later became something fundamental also for SQL.

Binary data type is a type of data where you can define a column as Binary and also

Specify the number of bytes that you want your column to hold.

Binary variable data type it's being used when the length of a variable is a variable.

Binary Large Object data type this type of data type is used when you are dealing with very very large binary strings that can't be processed with Binary type. Here we are talking about images, music files, any sort of audio files, video files, text documents and the list can go on and on. Binary large object data behaves a lot like ordinary binary strings but when working with them you will find out that SQL adds a big number of restrictions for any sort of action.

Date-times is a type of data that deals with multiple dates and times they also are being called date-time data and can be overlapped among the rest of four data types that we talked earlier.

Booleans, well the Booleans is representing a data type that has to deal with values. An affirmation receives 3 values: Trues, False and Unknown. It will give an Unknown value when one of those two values it's being compared with NULL.

Date data type is representing a data type that stores years, months and day values. The year is four digits long and the rest of the values are 2 digits long.

Intervals, the intervals data types are very closely to the date time data types. In fact the intervals are representing a difference between two date time values. Intervals are being used in applications where you have to deal with dates and different periods of time.

When working with SQL you will discover that the language recognizes two major types of intervals:

1. The first type of interval that we are going to discuss is "the year-month" interval. This interval is representing the number of years and months between two dates.
2. The second type of interval is "the day-time" interval and this is interval refers to a number specific number of days, hours, minutes and also seconds between two events within a month – period of time.

XML Type

XML is an abbreviation and it stands for eXtensible Markup Language and as the name sais is a markup language like HTML or CSS for example(do not confuse with programming languages). XML is a markup language that structures the data in a way that is very easy to understand and to use and also makes possible sharing between different platforms that the markup language it's being used.

When talking about the structure of XML data type it's very important to take in consideration the following thing : his structure is like a tree, so basically if thinking about a tree you will start thinking about the root of the tree and in this case the root is a node that has child nodes which also have child nodes. It's a "ramification" that was originally introduced in SQL: 2003 and augmented later in SQL:2008.

Let's talk about structure, the primary modifiers are Sequence, Content and Document and the secondary modifiers are UNTYPED Any, XMLSCHEMA.

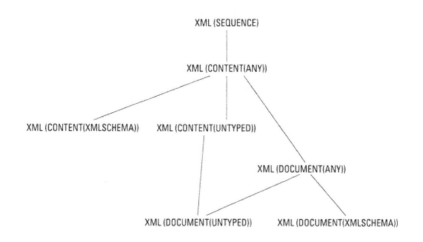

XML(Sequence): Values are either an SQL NULL value or XQuery (XQuery = query language designed to extract information from XML data) sequence. The XML (Sequence) is one of the most less restrictive of the XML types because it accepts values that are not well-formed.

XML(CONTENT(ANY)): this data type is representing a data type more restrictive than the first one XML(Sequence) for the fact that XML(Content(Any)) is representing an instance of XML (SEQUENCE) and can be described as a child of that node document.

XML(Content(UNTYPED)) : going down the list we find more and more restrictive data types, XML(Content (UNTYPED)) is a data type that is more restrictive than XML(Any Content).As we said earlier every XML value is either a NULL value or a non-null value.

XML(CONTENT(XMLSCHEMA)): Here we are talking about the second subtype of XML (Content(Any)) expecting XML (CONTENT(UNTYPED)).

XML(DOCUMENT(ANY)) : Another subtype of XML (CONTENT (ANY)) type that has a restriction applied. Instances of XML(Document(Any)) are representing nodes and they have just on XQuery element.

XML(Document(UNTYPED)): for this data type every single value is representing a NULL value or if not NON-NULL value of type XML(Content(UNTYPED)) and that is XQUERY document node whose children property has exactly one XQUERY element node.

ROW Types data

This type of data was introduced for the first time in SQL:1999. About this type of data we can say that it's pretty easy to understand and to use and as when you are just starting out you may not use it as you start out with SQL .As a matter of fact even though was introduced for a while this type of data didn't had been used a lot.

ARRAY Types

Is representing a data type is a Collection Type of data, not a distinct type of data but in the same sense that Character and Numeric type are. An Array is a type of data that allows one of the other types to have more values within a single field of a table.

MULTISET Type

A type of data that is representing an unordered collection. It has specific elements that might not be referenced because many of the elements are not assigned to any specific positions.

REF Types

We are talking about a type of data that it's not part of SQL, so as a result, we can say that a DBMS can claim compliance with SQL standard. REF Type is not a distinct data type like Character and Numeric type.

User-defined types

User-defined types represent another type of data that we are dealing with that presents a couple of features that came with SQL:1999 and we can say that it's a bridge that is being made with OOP (object oriented programming) world. When programming in SQL you are not restricted by the data types in SQL . In SQL you can define you own data types and by using principles of abstract data type found also in object oriented programming languages.

User defined types of data have different attributes and methods. Access to the attributes and methods can be made in the following ways :

- Public : available to all user defined types
- Private: available only to the user defined types itself
- Protected: available only for user defined types itself and for subtypes

Distinct types

Are representing a very simple type of data. A distinct type of data has a key feature : it's expressed as a single data type. It is constructed from one of the predefined data types called "source type".

Structured types

This is the second form of user-defined type , the structured type and is expressed as a list of attributes, definitions and methods.

Here we encounter a notion that comes from Object oriented programming and that is "Constructors". When we create a structured user-defined type of data, the DMBS creates also a constructor function and it's giving the same name as the user-defined type. His job is just to "initialize" the attributes.

Sub-types and Super-types = between Subtypes and Supertypes is creating a subordination relationship or hierarchical that can exist between structured types. As an example, we can have DirectorDit having a subtype named ActorDit. Also is important to specify that a structured type that doesn't have any Supertype is called Maximal Supertype and structured type that doesn't have any subtypes is called a Leaf Subtype.

Below you have attached a table with various data types that are displaying literals that conform for each type.

Data Type	Example Value
CHARACTER (20)	'Amateur Radio '
VARCHAR (20)	'Amateur Radio'
CLOB (1000000)	'This character string is a million characters long . . .'
SMALLINT, BIGINT, or INTEGER	7500
NUMERIC or DECIMAL	3425.432
REAL, FLOAT, or DOUBLE PRECISION	6.626E-34
BINARY (1)	'01100011'
VARBINARY (4)	'0110001111000110111100110'
BLOB (1000000)	'1001001110101011010101010101. . .'
BOOLEAN	'TRUE'
DATE	DATE '1957-08-14'
TIME (2) WITHOUT TIME ZONE [1]	TIME '12:46:02.43' WITHOUT TIME ZONE
TIME (3) WITH TIME ZONE	TIME '12:46:02.432-08:00' WITH TIME ZONE

NULL Values

Let's say a database field contains a data item and that field let's say has a specific value. We call it a "null value" a field that doesn't have any data item.

There are two big conditions that have to be met for that:

- A null value is not the same as with a value of zero, when talking about numeric field
- A null value is not the same with a blank, when talking about a character field

Either we are talking about zero or blank characters they both are definite values. Null values usually indicate that a field's value is unknown.

For that are a couple of situations that take place and the following list describers a couple of those situations:

- The value exists, but you don't know what the value is (yet).
- The field isn't applicable for this particular row
- The value is out of range
- The value doesn't exist or is not created (yet).

Constraints

Constraints are representing restrictions that are being applied to the values or data that a user can add into a database created in SQL.

In general, the application program that uses the database apply any constraints to a database. DBMS products enable you to apply constraints directly to your database.

Client/SERVER System in SQL

I'm pretty sure that till now we got clear the idea that SQL is a data sublanguage that can work on a multiuser system or standalone system. Users have access to multiple "client machines" on this type of systems to connect to a server machine through LAN (Local area network). This type of application program has SQL data manipulation commands and has a part of the DBMS that is residing on the client who sends commands to the server across the communication channel that is being used to connect from the server to the client. When the information arrives at the server it's being interpreted by the DBMS and then will start executing the SQL command and the interpretation will be sent back to the client through the communication channel. Here we have one of the most effective methods for communicating with the client and server.

The Server does nothing, the server has the role to stand and wait till has commands to process. If clients take the decision to ask for service then the server will come into action and It's supposed to react and response as quick as possible. We are supposing that the server will react fast (sometimes depending on other conditions it's not delivering the result in the shortest time possible, excepted situations) because of the fact that they have large amounts of fast storage and they are constantly optimized for this specific task, to be fast.

When talking about the server I consider to be very important to understand what the server it is and represents what the server isn't. The server must be very clear that is a part of client/server system and he has the role in holding the database(imagine the fact that here we are talking about very big databases and without then the database will not be working and the whole business/situation depends on the server quality, optimization and so on). Also when talking about the server it's important to have in mind that the server holds the server software also which is representing that part of the database management that has the role in interpreting commands that are coming in from the clients and to translate the commands into operations back to the database.

A server has a pretty simple and direct job because the server has the following tasks: receive the command, read the command, interpret the command and execute the command that comes to it from the client. Pretty simple job, right? It's important also to specify that the commands are coming in one of the several data sub languages (SQL).

The client also has a very important role in the relationship client/server. The client is the part that deals with the hardware competent in this situation and also the software component. To get a little bit deeper we going to say that the hardware component is representing the hardware component and is the client computer and its interface to the local area network.

What is the client and what is his role? Well it's pretty simple, the client's main task is to provide a user interface. Till now I'm pretty sure that everything it's clear, as far as user concerns the client machine is represented by the computer and the user interface is representing the application.

The client is supposed to represent the part of a DBMS that will display information on a screen and will reply to user input that is being transmitted through the peripheral equipment (mouse and keyboard). The client also will process data coming from any telecommunications links on the network.

Chapter 3 – The components of SQL

At the end of this chapter will be able to:

- Understand and create also databases
- Understand data manipulation
- How to protect databases

SQL is designed for creating and maintaining data in relational databases. Vendors of relational database management system developed their own SQL methods of implementation, ISO/IEC standard that define and control the whole purpose of SQL and activity.

SQL, as we discussed till now, is not a programming language, although it contains a lot of characteristics reminding to a programming language and also has some impressive tools. SQL has tree languages integrated that are offering to the programmer everything he needs when it comes to creating, maintaining or modifying data for a relational database:

1. DDL (Data definition language) is the first one that we are going to talk about. DDL is that part of SQL that creates

the database and also modifies the structure of it and at the end deletes parts of it or the entire database when is no longer need it.

2. DML(Data manipulation Language) is the second part that performs maintenance for your SQL database, also for making changes, entering or removing informations.

3. DCL(Data control language) is the third part of SQL and this part has the purpose to protect and secure the database that you created from becoming corrupted. Data control language offers to your database the amount of security that needs if it's being created correctly and also used correctly.

Now we are going to talk more detailed about each part of SQL about their purpose how to use it and so on.

Data definition language

Data definition language as we said earlier has the purpose to create, modify and also to destroy some components of a relational database. Some components or elements that we can include are tables, catalogs, schemes and so on. Tables and schemas are structures that contain tables within their structure, they contain a containment hierarchy in the relational databases, so we have the following hierarchy:

- Tables have columns and rows
- Schemas have tables and views

When thinking about planning a database let's talk about a couple of points that you should consider:

- Start by identifying all tables that you want to include in your database
- Create and define the columns of your database
- Assign a *primary key* for every table. Don't worry will get later into "primary key" subject

Let's create a **table.** The table from our database should look a lot like a spreadsheet table. To be more specific, a two-dimensional array that is made up of rows and columns. The command that you have to use to create a SQL table is CREATE Table. When using the command you have to specify also the name and data type for each column you add in your database. Once you created the table you can start working on it and entering all the information's that you are interested. When you originally created your table didn't include something that you wanted or want to change the structure you can do it very easy by using the command ALTER TABLE.

Multi-table view – you can create a multi-table view to show you the data that you are interested in.

DDL statements – Data definition language has only three statements

1. First one is CREATE – this command is being used to build the essential structure of the database and many other forms
2. The second one is ALTER – this command has the purpose of changing structures that you originally made or want to add something new to what you have created.
3. The third one is DROP – this command you have to apply to structures created with the command CREATE and to delete/destroy the structure previously created.

CREATE

"CREATE" command can be used in SQL with a lot of different purposes and can be applied to many SQL objects, tables and so on. "CREATE SCHEMA" it's being used to create a schema in your database and also to identify a character set.

ALTER

"ALTER" command can be used also to discover if everything it's ok with your database and everything it's working properly. "ALTER TABLE" is a statement that can be used to change the table modifying / deleting informations.

DROP

"DROP" command has the purpose of removing a table from your database in a very simple way. "DROP TABLE" command will erase all data from your table.

Data Manipulation Language

DML or data manipulation language is that part of SQL that handles and takes care of data in SQL, as we talked earlier DDL or data definition language is the part of SQL that deals with creating or modifying or deleting different parts and structures from your database.

Data manipulation language includes in their "arsenal" multiple types of statements or expressions to use when working. After start working with them, you will soon get to the conclusion that is not that hard to use. While talking about statements that can be used we can enumerate very easy the following: INSERT, UPDATE, SELECT, DELETE, MERGE and will take care o each one. Each statement can incorporate "value expressions" and also logical expressions, function expressions.

Let's talk about "**Value Expressions**". We can use value expressions to combine two or more values when working. Below will have a list of several kinds of value expressions that we usually work with and are linked to different data types:

- String
- Date time
- Numeric
- Interval
- Row
- Collection
- User-defined
- Boolean

Numeric value expressions

When talking about numeric value expressions it's very important to talk about how to use addition (+) and subtraction (-) in combining numeric values. Also multiplication (*) and division (/) are representing another operators that we have to work with and to bring into the discussion.

String value expressions

String value expressions include concatenation operators like (||) that are being used to join text strings.

Date time / Interval value expressions

Let's start with date time expressions, they have to deal with dates and times when working with them. Here we can enumerate a couple of very known statements like : date of TIME, TIME, TIMESTRAMP that are considered to be date time expressions. What results from a date-time expression is always and always another date time and as a result you can add or remove an interval from a date time or different time information's.

Interval value expressions it has to work with how much time has passed and how has been processed the difference of time between one date time to another date time. Here we have to remind two types of intervals that we can work with :

- Year month interval
- Day time interval

Boolean value expressions

Boolean value expressions have the purpose of testing the truth value of an expression. Let's look at the following example:

(Andrew = STUDENT) IS TRUE

In the example above we can see that we have a condition on the retrieval of rows.

User-defined type value expressions

A couple of expressions that we can talk about are expressions that incorporate data elements like the following:

- Row value expressions
- Collection value expressions = are representing a collection value expression that evaluates to an array
- Reference value expressions = are representing a value expression that evaluates to a value that references some other data-base component

Predicates

Predicates are representing in SQL the equivalent of logical propositions. For example Andrew = STUDENT is a comparison predicate. SQL has 6 comparison operators. Below you have a table with the comparison operators and comparison predicates

Operator	Comparison
=	Equal to
<>	Not equal to
<	Less than
>	Greater than
<=	Less than or equal to
>=	Greater than or equal to

Logical connectives

We use logical connectives to build or create complex predicates(expecting the simple predicates).

Set functions

Depending on how the task you have looks like you may be in the situation that you may have to extract data from a table that doesn't really relate to individual rows but rather to sets of rows. SQL provides the following functions to deal with in those type of situations : COUNT, MAX, MIN, SUM, AVG. Each of those functions performs an action that "windows" data from a set of rows rather tan from a single row.

COUNT FUNCTION

The COUNT function it is a function that has the purpose to return the number of rows in the specified table.

MAX FUNCTION

The MAX function works in the following way: returns the maximum values that occur in the specified column.

MIN Function

The MIN function works very similar to MAX function but a single exception: MIN function is developed to look for the minimum value in the selected field (or column) than the maximum.

SUM Function

The SUM function it has the purpose of adding values to a selected column. The column that can get new values must be one of the numeric data types and the value of the SUM has to be within the range of that type.

AVG Function

The AVG function has the role in returning the AVERAGE for the values that are being selected in a specific field. AVG function always is applied to columns with a numeric data type.

Data Control Language

The data control language or DCL has the following commands: COMMIT, ROLLBACK, GRANT, REVOKE.

SQL protects your database by adding restricting operations (your database is very vulnerable or fragile when a user is modifying it or making any kind of change) to change your database and as a result transactions can occur. If anything appears into the transaction to interrupt it, the COMMIT statement is being used to end the transaction and if you have to restore the system all you have to do it's to use the ROLLBACK statement.

When talking about privileges another threat for your database integrity is the persons or users that have access to information and that it's representing one of the most vulnerable aspects of your database. Some users should not have access to your database at all due to bad intentions and so on or limited access. For this type of situations SQL has been designed to give you the capacity to protect the following objects in your database so your work would not be destroyed by a person:

- Tables
- Columns
- Views
- Domains
- Character sets
- Collations
- Translations

When it comes to protection SQL offers the support on different kinds of protection like: seeing, adding, modifying, deleting, and referencing databases.

Types of protection

Protection operation	Statement
Enable user to see a table	GRANT SELECT
Prevent user from seeing a table	REVOKE SELECT
Enable user to add rows to a table	GRANT INSERT
Prevent user from adding rows to a table	REVOKE INSERT
Enable user to change data in table rows	GRANT UPDATE
Prevent user from changing data in table rows	REVOKE UPDATE
Enable user to delete table rows	GRANT DELETE
Prevent user from deleting table rows	REVOKE DELETE
Enable user to reference a table	GRANT REFERENCES
Prevent user from referencing a table	REVOKE REFERENCES
Enable user to use a domain, character set, translation, or collation	GRANT USAGE ON DOMAIN, GRANT USAGE ON CHARACTER SET, GRANT USAGE ON COLLATION, GRANT USAGE ON TRANSLATION
Prevent user from using a domain, character set, collation, or translation	REVOKE USAGE ON DOMAIN, REVOKE USAGE ON CHARACTER SET, REVOKE USAGE ON COLLATION, REVOKE USAGE ON TRANSLATION

Building and Maintaining a Simple Database Structure

Now we are going to take a view on how to build and also maintain a simple database structure by learning how to:

- Use RAD for your database
- Use SQL for your database and migrate to DBMS

Due to the fact that SQL is not a complete programming language and deals with databases, SQL it doesn't fit in the general programming languages that we know. SQL has to be used with the conjunction with an IDE or older generation development tools.

When using **RAD** tools to build databases you have to keep track of important information's to know what you have to have in attention for your project. From time to time information that you want to pick up happen to be very simple but also can happened to be very complicated to be used. When talking about a good database management system we talk about a system that provides what you need either you have very simple information to work with or complicated information.

From the start of your project you have to decide on what you are going to track and constant look on, it's on of the first steps that you have to take. Once you decided on what type of information's you what to track you can easily start working, your tracking information's could easily look like:

- First name
- Last name
- Address
- Country

- Age
- Phone

If we are trying to create a database to store information's about individuals that keep information's like name, location age and so on.

Building a database with SQL's DDL – database definition functions can perform very good with RAD Tools (here we can talk for example about Microsoft Access that can be easily used for creating databases) are also possible to be used even if your are using SQL to build a table.

SQL can be used with Microsoft Access because is designed as a rapid application development tool and this application doesn't require programming. SQL statements can be very easy be written in Microsoft Access(even though you can rule the code to get the result and just write, create and store your tables) and also you will have to use a back-door method. In future chapters with talk more about database creation and also will talk about portability considerations. That any SQL implementation you may want to use can be very easy ported to another platform or from a platform to another platform, making your job even easier.

Chapter 4: Building a multi-table relational database

At the end of this chapter will be able to:

- What is necessary and unnecessary to include in your database when start working on it
- What type of relationships are among data items and how to determine relationship
- How to design or redesign your database for data integrity
- And much much more

We are going to talk about how to design a multi-table databases and one of the first steps that you have to have in consideration before starting to work on a new database is to identify on what to include in your database and what not to include in your database as we talked at the end of the previous chapter and also will get in depth in the process of database creation.

Let's start designing a database

1. Start by deciding the objects that you want your database to have
2. Define tables on how you want and also need to structure your objects in your database

Defining objects is one of the first things that I recommend to do when start working on your database and also decide what elements are important to your database as soon as you are just starting out, also as long as you are creating objects in your database I recommend you to strat creating lists with the most relevant objects that you have and need in your database but your decisions don't have to be permanent at this point due to the fact that you are just starting out developing your project.

A table has columns and rows. Identifying your columns in your table is another important step that you have to do and to be sure that you have designed all columns that you need in your database (name, address, phone number, e-mail and so on, depending on what your database needs)

The crucial element lies on how you Define now your table for each entity and also a column for each attribute.

Getting into your database fast with keys = It's not important for you to design your database just your columns but also your rows and each of rows that you are designing must be unique and properly created. For example, will be moments when you will need quick access to information in your database with the purpose of extracting them and in order to do that you will need to have very specific rows created and to eliminate all the unnecessary rows that your table may contain.

What is a primary key and what is the purpose of it?

Well, a *primary key* is nothing more than a column in your table with values that identify different rows created in your table. The primary key was the purpose to be incorporated with the rest of access keys in your table . The Primary Key also has the purpose of replacing the constraint NOT NULL.

A foreign key is representing a column or group of columns in your table that makes reference to your primary key. Your foreign key doesn't have to be a unique element, all it has to do is to identify specific columns in your tables where references are being made.

SQL references don't have to be addressed on specific topics when working with indexes per say. When talking about SQL implementation supports indexes are very important and everything that is related to working with indexes.

But meanwhile what is an index and what an index does? Well it's pretty simple, data, in general, appears in a table that you created in the order that has been entered first time(that order has nothing related with how it will be arranged later) You want to process STUDENT in table StudentNameOrder, your computer firstly has to understand how to sort data, and order StudentNameOrder, this is a very time consuming process.

It is very important to understand that that indexing is a process that helps you a lot because if you use an index you can perform your operations of arranging and ordering very fast, almost as fast as you could if the data table itself were already in StudentNameOrder order.

Maintenance of an index is very easy, you don't have to think a lot about that and pay a lot of attention because of your DBMS. DBMS maintains your indexes automatically by making updates to your index every time you are updating your corresponding data tables, yes might be time consuming, yes might be tiring but is very useful and worth for sure.

Tip: a very good moment to create an index is at the same time on create it's corresponding data table.

Maintaining data integrity is a very important topic, data integrity means making sure that any data that you enter into your database system satisfied the constraints that have been established.

Cascading deletions – you can eliminate most problems that are related to integrity problems by taking a good care of what controls the update process. In the most cases the cascade deletions it's being made from a parent table to its children. For a cascade deletion you will delete a row from a parent table and also you will delete all the rows in the child tables (and their foreign keys that match with the primary key of the deleted row in the parent table)

Be sure that you are keeping everything safe! At the end, you will have created a database with tables and constraints and so on. The worst thing that can happen is to have a bad database management because everything will finally collapse and your work will be useless.

Constraints = A constraint is an application rule that the DBMS enforces.

There are three kinds of constraints that we can talk about:

- A column constraint = imposes a condition on a column
- A table constraint = adds a specified constraint on the entire table
- An assertion = constant that affects more than one table

Normalizing your database

There are more ways in which you can normalize your database, some of them better, some worst, some are more logical and some simpler. Normalizing it's necessary due to the fact that every time you modify your database you open your database for a lot of troubles and challenges and a search for solutions also.

We are going to have a little talk about first normal form and how after you normalize your database as much as possible you will probably make selected de-normalizations to improve performance

First Normal form = to have a first normal form (1NF) a table must meet the following:

- Two-dimensional table with rows and columns
- Rows must contains data that pertains to some thing
- Columns must have a single attribute
- Each cell of your table should have a single value
- In your columns must be unique names
- Order it's not relevant

Conclusion

Thank you again for downloading this book!

I hope this book was able to help you to understand how to work with SQL and to create databases and also enjoyed the book!

The next step is to be sure that you fully understand the information, also apply it and read it as frequently as necessary.

Finally, if you enjoyed this book, then I'd like to ask you for a favour, would you be kind enough to leave a review for this book on Amazon? It'd be greatly appreciated!

If you enjoyed the the this book check out other releases that you might like:

Data Analytics: Essentials to master Data Analytics and get your business to the next level

Passive Income: 3 Proven Business Models That Generate Online Revenue to Achieve Financial Freedom

www.ingramcontent.com/pod-product-compliance
Lightning Source LLC
Chambersburg PA
CBHW070902070326
40690CB00009B/1951